EVOLUTION AUTISTIC

Unveiling
the
Real Reasons Behind Autism

A Parents Guide

NICOLE KRETSCHMANN

EVOLUTION AUTISTIC

Unveiling the Real Reasons Behind Autism

A Parents Guide

Copyright © Nicole Kretschmann

First published 2024

ISBN: 978-1-7635558-2-2 Book

ISBN: 978-1-7635558-3-9 E-Book

ISBN: 978-1-7635558-4-6 Audio

All rights reserved. Without limiting the rights under copyright reserved above, no part of this publication may be reproduced, stored in or introduced into a database and retrieval system or transmitted in any form or by any means (electronic, mechanical, photocopying, recording or otherwise) without the prior written permission of the owner of the copyright.

> Disclaimer: The author and persons associated with the publishing and distributing of this book accepts no liability should any unforeseen circumstances occur, including that of a detrimental nature to anyone as a direct result of reading this book. The medical information provided within this book's content is general and cannot substitute for professional medical advice, diagnosis, or treatment. Always seek the advice of your physician or other qualified health professional with any questions you may have regarding a medical condition. All information supplied has no warranty whatsoever. Information and statements are not intended to treat, cure, or prevent disease. All information in this book, including information about medical and health conditions, products and treatments, is for informational purposes only. It is often presented in summary or aggregate form.

Published with the assistance of Angel Key Publications
https://angelkey.com.au

Contents

DEDICATIONS. v

EVOLUTION AUTISTIC. vii

Chapter 1
AUTISM DIAGNOSIS 1

Chapter 2
THE D WORDS. 5

Chapter 3
EVOLUTION 9

Chapter 4
SPIRITUALITY. 13

Chapter 5
SCHOOL. 19

Chapter 6
SENSES 21

Chapter 7
HYPER VERSUS HYPO 25

Chapter 8
TELEPATHY 27

Chapter 9
REGULATE THE NERVOUS SYSTEM 35

Chapter 10
PANS 39

Chapter 11
FUNDING 41

Chapter 12
THE 5TH DIMENSION 45

CONCLUSION 51

ABOUT THE AUTHOR 53

Notes 54

DEDICATIONS

Dedicated to my four beautiful sons; thank you for being my teachers in this lifetime. It didn't start with you and certainly won't end with you. Thank you for shaping the world and bringing a higher intelligence and calibration to Earth.

*To my husband, thank you for your endless love, support,
and belief in me.*

I extend my heartfelt thanks to the guiding force of Universal source energy and intelligence and for the continuous support and downloads throughout my journey. It has brought me to this present moment of my life, revealing evidence of where we are collectively heading. A special thank you to Archangel Michael and my guides.

*For those lost and misunderstood consciousnesses in human form who have always felt like they didn't belong-
Own your powers, tune in and lead the way.*

EVOLUTION AUTISTIC

Embracing the positive journey of neuro differences, spiritually, scientifically, and evolutionally.

'A book crafted for parents of autistic children, shedding light on the positive attributes of these remarkable individuals'.

I was called to write this book by a higher intelligence. My story is somewhat different. I gave birth to my first child in 2017, and something inside me changed. I was gifted with a source connection, with the ability to go beyond the five human senses. He changed my consciousness and my connection with the universal source. I didn't know what was happening to me at that time. All I knew was that I could see, hear and feel things I hadn't been able to before his existence. Some would label this insane. I now know it connected me to other dimensions. I will be forever grateful to Marco, who mentored me through the journey and allowed me to explore my gifts and connect to others no longer in the physical.

I feel I have a duty to society to present a different view on autism, I'm prepared to be met initially with scepticism. However, it is what I know to be true and in which I have complete faith. It will benefit society if we all can understand why these special humans are here and what we need to learn from them, and not continue to place limiting beliefs on them and their parents. Allow them the space, love, and compassion to become their fully expanded version.

This book comes with many purposes. One is the reassurance to parents of young autistic children that it's okay and that it's going to be okay. Your child is still the same, and your love for them will never change. There will be hard days, and your child needs you, so be strong. When you have it hard, remember your child has it harder. An autism diagnosis is not there to change who they are; it's to help you understand why they think and act differently from what you were taught and why they feel things so much more intensely. It also serves as the reason why you cannot parent them as you've been led to believe. They are also not here to fit into society's box; they will help you realise there is no box and never was.

Chapter 1

AUTISM DIAGNOSIS

Congratulations. Let's celebrate. You or someone you know have been blessed with an autism diagnosis. This person has gifts beyond your understanding and is here to teach you.

How you choose to receive, integrate and embody this knowledge is a personal choice based on what level of Evolution you are already at and that which you are still to call into your life. What you believe about your child, and their limits and or limitless, is what you will push into your reality. The best advice I can give you, which I wish was given to me, is to embody the positive elements of your child and ignore the negative elements that are deemed negative by man-made measures.

I remember the day my son's paediatrician said to me, "I'm sorry, it is autism". I'm sorry? She's apologising to me for the way my son is? So many thoughts went through my mind. Why is she sorry? What kind of journey am I about to embark on? Why has this happened? What did I do wrong? Oh my god, he's never going to lead a regular life, and this will be so hard.

Looking back, I realise that my thoughts were just fears of the unknown. I knew my boy had some big emotions. I knew his anxiety level was off the charts. I knew he was meant to be talking, but he wasn't. I knew he was highly sensitive to energies, seen and unseen. He communicated in a different style. He didn't like being in unfamiliar places. He couldn't go to daycare or be without his parents. He was still such a sweet, empathetic soul, just beautiful inside and out, but she's saying, "I'm sorry". I must have it all wrong.

I wish I could turn back the time and celebrate his diagnosis, scream it, advertise it, tell anyone who would listen, and above all be grateful, be grateful we were given one of the special ones. Be thankful that he chose me to mother him. Caring for such an evolved being is an honour and a privilege.

To other parents on this journey, I want you to remember this on the days you question everything. These children were entrusted to you, to you alone. It is you they yearn for, you who possess the very essence they require. In the face of adversity, you radiate an unwavering love that envelops them on the most challenging days. Your dedication and boundless affection empower you to provide every necessity in a world that often overlooks their extraordinary gifts. With a heart full of unwavering determination, you rise each day, prepared to embrace it all over again, no matter the exhaustion that looms. Your smile is their heart's desire, and your touch can miraculously heal and regulate. To them, you are the Universe that soothes their souls. Never wish that away or take it for granted.

Once you release the energy of victimisation and embrace the energy of anticipation, watch your life change for the better. The challenge is the curriculum for life, not the curriculum for school. Universal curriculum versus man-made curriculum: know the difference, operate and make decisions for your child while young, honouring the universal curriculum.

You've come here to learn; they've come here to teach.

Chapter 2

THE D WORDS

Neurodivergence, in general, is not a negative thing. Each altered neurotype has a spiritual definition and a greater purpose in coming through in this lifetime with an atypical operating system.

An autism diagnosis comes with a lot of outdated and inaccurate dialogue. Some of the words you may come across that need disregarding are:

Disability — labelled by those who don't understand.

Deficit — labelled by those unevolved opinions

Disorder — everything is in perfect order!

These words and patterns of thinking or viewing autism need to be realigned and renewed. Replace them with:

Determined — to what matters.

Dedicated — to the ones they love.

Dynamic — energetic and lively.

Deliberate — everything is planned.

Decisive — don't ask them to change their minds.

Distinguished — recognised unique gifts.

Devoted — loyal beyond words.

Driven — commonly labelled as fixated interests.

Dazzling — look into their eyes.

Differentiated — no two souls are the same.

Autistic kids are like truth-tellers; they say it how it is, with no filters and no pretending. If what they're saying makes you uncomfortable, that's on you, not them. It's a chance to learn from their perspective and celebrate their authenticity. Instead of trying to change them, let's embrace their honesty—it makes relationships real.

Now, there's this big misconception about empathy and compassion. People think autistic kids lack it, but that's far from true. They often feel deeply for others, maybe even more than we do, because they see the world differently. But sometimes, it all gets too much, and they must switch off for a while. It's not that they don't care; it's just their way of coping. So, if they're not vibing with someone, there's a reason. As a parent, it's crucial to respect that and not push them into uncomfortable situations. Let them choose who they connect with—they'll thrive better.

Now let's talk about their talents! These kids are like superstars in fields like tech, math, music, art—you name it. Their laser focus and attention to detail are what set them apart. As we dive deeper into the digital era, these kids will lead the charge, shaping our future with their incredible minds. So, let's listen up and learn from them. They've got a lot to teach us!

We're diving headfirst into the world of Artificial Intelligence, whether we're ready or not. And you know who will be at the forefront of this digital revolution? These amazing kids. Providing we nurture their gifts, not beat them out of them. Let them have all the technology in the world without restrictions. They're like the pioneers of a whole new era, showing us what's possible with their unique minds. Think about it: these kids are like the next level of intelligence. They're pushing the boundaries of what we thought was possible for the human brain. It's like witnessing Evolution in real time. So, let's embrace it. Let's recognise that these kids are the key to unlocking a future we can't imagine yet. They're not just kids but the architects of tomorrow's world, and we're lucky to be along for the ride.

It always blows my mind how they label these kids as delayed just because they don't hit certain milestones at a certain age. Who has the right to decide that? These man-made measures aren't useful. But when you see an autistic child memorise a book after reading it once or fix the electronics on a washing machine at age five, nobody calls the neurotypical child delayed because they can't do that. It's the height of double standards and a set of standardised terms to put us in a box again.

The thing is, the scope of our children's abilities isn't limited to what society expects at a certain age. It's not like their future is set in stone based on these arbitrary standards. They're so much more than that. Let's ditch the labels and let them show us what they're truly capable of. Their potential is limitless, and I'm here, showing up for every bit. Be that parent.

Chapter 3

EVOLUTION

There are many unconfirmed autistic neurotypes in our world. These individuals, mainly adults, often struggle with day-to-day life. They may not have had parents who understood their needs and instead were labelled as 'lazy, naughty, or stupid.' Their passions and interests may have diminished because they were not 'socially accepted', with parents caring more about others' opinions than their children's happiness.

One of the best hairdressers I have ever met was a man from Scotland. He is autistic, and his passion is haircutting. His methods are precise and immaculate. He grew up in a household where his passions and sexuality were not accepted. He was strong enough to leave his country and family to find his purpose in Australia. Today, he is a successful, award-winning hairdresser with a thriving business. His clients have become like family, and he brings endless love and laughter to those who seek his services, boosting their self-confidence and raising their spirits. Those who visit him love and accept his quirks, appreciating him for who he truly is. Following his passion led him to his loving partner, who was also a hairdresser.

I have endless compassion for those who didn't survive their childhoods with their gifts intact. Many were pressured to 'fit in' and 'act normal,' pushing them off the path of their dreams because it was considered 'weird.' Many weren't born into accepting households or had mentors who could embrace them for who they were. Autistic children know they are different and understand their purpose, but years of conditioning can break them. Constant punishment for not conforming can stifle their potential. Please don't make the same mistake with your children. By doing so, you are hindering their Evolution and universal purpose.

Let's look at the confirmed numbers. In 2000, 1 in 150 children were diagnosed as autistic. In 2024, the year I am writing this, the number has increased to 1 in 36 children. I predict that beyond 2055, we will see an even distribution of autistic and neurotypical brain wiring—50% autistic and 50% neurotypical. Can you imagine a world where autistics lead? They are labelled as 'weird' because they are not understood and outnumbered. In the future, we might describe neurotypicals in ways that highlight their differences, showing how easily the script can be flipped.

On a side note, if your child isn't interested in socialising, please don't force them. The day will come when they choose or feel ready to interact, but if they don't, let them be. Allow them to stay in their own world; they need this time to complete their life purpose.

Many theories are attempting to link the increase in autism to parenting, genetics, disability schemes, or the environment, but there are no solid answers. It's time to accept that this is how humans are destined to evolve and prepare for what's coming. Imagine a world where, instead of teaching autistic individuals how to interact with others, we focus on teaching those without autism how to connect with autistics. The world is changing, and autistic dominance is on the horizon.

We are entering a new era for humanity that many struggle to accept. How often have you heard, "Why are there so many autistic kids these days?" or "There were no autistic children in my day" or even "These children just need some good discipline; it's their parents' fault?" These statements reflect resistance to change. The increase in autism is not due to the conditions speculated; it's simply the dawn of a new era.

Get ready for a future where autistic individuals are accepted and celebrated. We will witness more and more autistic calibrations incarnating, and soon, they will dominate. This shift promises a vibrant, diverse world where new ways of thinking and being will flourish. Embrace the excitement of this new era and anticipate the incredible contributions and collective increase in vibrational fields that autistic individuals will bring to our evolving society.

The Earth is also going through an ascension process and evolving. It's a vibration of love and light. Similar to heaven on Earth. You may have seen many of the spiritual teachers speaking about the 5th dimension. A genuine shift is happening on Earth, and these children are here to assist with the transition.

Chapter 4

SPIRITUALITY

I have been shown and know many more of these beautiful children are coming.

I want you to know this book is here to support you and allow you the support or the permission you need to enable them to own their powers and step into their gifts to propel them on their spiritual journey and possibly yours. I will hold true to my faith and belief and my higher power in knowing and sharing the knowledge of why they are here.

I can see a vast, world-changing vision. I am being called to share it. A new free, empowered earth, a new free and empowered humanity.

These children have heightened senses, and I speak to this as an evolutionary process. These children vibrate at such a high frequency. The misalignment comes from trying to fit this frequency into a human body. They must learn to combine the two. Many studies are showing psychic telepathy communications between autistic individuals and psychic mediums, who are also likely autistic, diagnosed or not.

What was the original intention of the source creating these kids? We shouldn't seek to change them or try to alter who they are because all this does is go against the flow of divine source and damage them individually. It'll also damage and exhaust you as a carer. They are here for a reason. Trust them that they have the power to create. They can and source energy wants them to. If they choose to create, and they will in one way or another, you can trust their judgment and support them wholeheartedly.

This is what I can see and feel as coming for humanity. Autistic children have many heightened emotions. It is part and parcel of the evolving human being and emotional structure. Those incarnated as autistic are often labelled as having a disability because of how most will display emotions. It can be misunderstood by professionals who are taught a particular structure around human behaviour.

These autistic individuals have very highly calibrated nervous systems. They are also so highly sensitive. On the other side of big emotions are those autistic individuals who 'lack emotions'. The view that these individuals do not have emotions is incorrect. They sometimes won't show emotion. That's a choice they are making. Sometimes, they will shut down simply for coping mechanisms, but they want to avoid it if they can. We hear a lot about female autistic masking; this is simply shutting down to cope with the intense emotion and the worry of punishment. Masking is just another term for faking being human. How sad is it to think they have to fake their incarnation because the rest of the world hasn't caught up? The nervous system is very refined and tailored to intensity. They are also in the field of high intelligence.

These children will be the ones to carry the world into a more highly evolved state and lead the way with humanity in this highly evolved state. I expect to see them leading the way to greater expanded consciousness, expanded energy fields and experience on the planet. The planet, as it is, is still learning about emotions and the interpretation of emotions. The autistic child, as they are, is still learning about how to be in this body—navigating and learning emotions linked to the physical body, yet on a higher state of consciousness. Let's look at what the future human looks like, as our choices and understanding will navigate how we get there. This notion of them being less has to end.

Many neurotypicals are curious about what happens when you have a more highly calibrated nervous system. What does this look like? Physically, higher energy calibration brings larger emotions to the surface. Sound and other sensory inputs can be particularly overwhelming for those with higher sensitivity. Navigating this in everyday environments often creates big emotions. But in this evolved state, the body is also changing. There's a metamorphosis happening to accept this advanced soul.

Significant changes and clashes occur as the soul's frequency enters the physical being. The dense physical body must adjust to the higher frequency of the soul, leading to many emotional, social, and sensory differences. This highly tuned nervous system allows access to greater creativity. This transformation isn't just about individual growth—it's about changing the Earth and beyond.

Even if you are only slightly in tune and a little aware, you can already feel the coming change. We are currently in a cycle of life where we are on the cusp of significant changes and new eras. We are experiencing the greatest spiritual awakening in human history. These kids can adapt to what is happening. In contrast, the less evolved will not be able to adjust to the new changes. We are moving beyond material concerns and stepping into higher realms of understanding.

Autistic people are connected to source energy. They see the big picture through their wisdom and insight. They know things we don't. These people act on their higher selves. The problems arise when they are dictated to or stopped from acting from their higher selves. You'll often see this in school. It'll go one of two ways—violent, aggressive, loud, angry behaviours or withdrawn anxious emotional behaviours.

Humans coming through in this century are full of genetic differences. This is planned. This is evolutionary. Know that there is a higher purpose to it. These children are often described as mechanical when verbal. Sure, they may sound this way to others, but they're trying to speak in a way that others will understand what they're talking about. They are enthusiastic about what they can bring to the planet and why they are here. Neurotypicals (NTs) label this behaviour as obsessive, over-the-top, or hyperactive, but it's the full force of quantum energy driving them to share their purpose.

What these children feel, sense, and know doesn't always come across well through language. There's always a difficulty with science trying to comprehend the spiritual aspects of humans that very few can understand. See the gifts and blessings in the challenges of life and the way these children push us to see, do, and be better. Humans in NT form are too focused on 'victimisation' and labelling these kids as disabled instead of recognising them as reincarnated in a higher frequency form.

Chapter 5

SCHOOL

If your child is expressing that they do not want to be in school and you're in a position to do so, please consider homeschooling your autistic child or at least look for part-time alternate schooling options. Foster a layer of safety and security around them and watch them thrive. You'll be glad you did. School for an autistic child is like navigating a circus. They must put 100% effort and energy into surviving a day in that overwhelming environment.

On top of that, parents, teachers, and peers expect them to learn, socialise, and 'behave'. Despite their tremendous and exhausting efforts, their results often fall short of those of their peers, and social acceptance is fleeting. This sets them up for painful comparisons and bitter frustration. Instead of being a fun and fulfilling experience, school can become a breeding ground for depression and anxiety, turning home into a battleground.

It's exhausting for everyone involved to send your autistic child to mainstream school. Keep them home. I'll have parents tell me, "But what about socialising them?" Let them decide. If they don't want to be social, that is okay. The digital era we are moving towards does not require such a skill. Let them be who they want to be. If they don't feel like being social, that's okay. As adults, many of us, autistic or otherwise, don't feel like being social for long periods. Let them be who they are; let them be happy. If they want to be social, they will be; otherwise, they are perfectly okay. Other children can inhibit the growth of the autistic child because kids will be kids, but inflicting chaos on the senses of your autistic child and creating havoc on their nervous system, intentional or not, will be to the detriment of your child.

We are moving into a new era. The way we communicate is changing. Let's move with their natural flow, not against them. Creativity comes effortlessly and easily. It signifies aligning with one's true self and higher purpose.

I often describe the placement of an autistic child into the mainstream education system like this: The issue with hammering a triangular peg into a circular hole is not just that the hammering is physically and mentally exhausting but that you are destroying the peg. Don't destroy your peg. There is a special light inside the soul of this child. Mainstream will diminish the light.

Through the progression of consciousness, we are creating a more beautiful, kinder, and loving world. It is happening. Embrace autistic children and treasure them. Autism and your child cannot be separated; they are autistic. Specific therapies aim to separate your child from their autism, trying to make them act 'neurotypical.' Do yourself and your child a favour and avoid these therapies and schools that promote these therapies at all costs.

Chapter 6

SENSES

These children are susceptible to their surroundings, including energies not physically detected through your sensory system. They take 'reading the room' to new levels, picking up and absorbing the energy of others. It makes negative environments or people with negative energies particularly challenging for them to be around. Trust and listen to them. Suppose they don't like a person or place, respect that. They feel and know much more than you do. These kids can gather vast amounts of information from their environment and others simply by reading energy with their senses. This heightened perception allows them to notice and appreciate subtle details that others may overlook, leading to a greater appreciation of beauty in the environment or unique problem-solving abilities. Since most are empaths, they feel things more intensely and can be easily triggered. Keep this in mind before judging them as too reactive.

It will be beneficial to create quiet, alone spaces where they feel comfortable and safe so they can download and communicate with universal powers. If they are drowned out, you cannot expect these kids to move forward with their work; by drowned out, I mean not given a chance to be in solitude, forced to socialise or placed in overwhelming environments. If they are uncomfortable or their behaviours are off the chart, get them away from the environment where they are. Give them peace. Give them solitude. Allow them to be in harmony. They will often seek out activities that will ground them. Allow them to explore their fixations. If that means eight hours of spinning a car wheel, let them do it. Trust me when I say they know what is best for them, to regulate their nervous system. We live in a culture with such odd, outdated beliefs, man-made beliefs, which don't serve these kids well. For example, we tend to feel sorry for the kid playing alone, 'look at that kid, so sad, so lonely'. If they are neurodiverse, they will be happy playing alone and will not require company to feel whole and complete. Let them be.

This brings me to the next subject of food! These kids come into the world with such a high vibration. They are highly reactive to how some earthly foods make their bodies feel. Most of them won't be keen on eating meat or dense, heavy meat. That is okay. Please don't force them. They will have restricted diets, which is fine; they need to vibrate energetically at a certain level. The reason a lot of autistic adults have lost their gifts over time as it was forced out of them. For many, the damage happened in their childhood, and they spend their adulthoods having to process and heal from the trauma. These days, we have more free will. Give your children the free will to decide their health and food intake. Vegan and vegetarian tendencies will come through. And if they don't feel like eating, don't force them; they may need to feel lighter in their bodies for spiritual purposes, and less food intake supports this feeling. I know this information is counterintuitive to everything we've been taught, but the thing is, what we've been taught doesn't apply to these kids. The aura that comes with these kids will mean allergies and sensitivities will also be heightened.

Regarding touching, particularly affection, it's best not to force these kids to hug or feel things they don't want to. They are sensitive to the vibrations of other human beings, animals, and physical objects. Certain vibrations are not good for their nervous systems, so they shy away. Certain humans are not good for their nervous systems, and they will shy away. Always respect their feelings and don't force anything. Forcing them past their vibrational alignment puts them out of whack with their calibrations. You will feel like parenting them is hard. It can be extra hard due to the things they are forced to endure. If you find this hard to believe, just try it. Let them make the decisions. Let them lead. Let them not be dictated to. Watch how quickly things change.

Sleep is often a problematic area for these kids. Besides needing safety and security, they also have trouble producing melatonin. My theory centres around the third eye and the pineal gland. When the pineal gland is in darkness, it produces melatonin. Many autistic kids are prescribed melatonin to help them sleep. People with a bright inner consciousness find it hard to contain this light within the standard human body. The human body will struggle to sleep if the pineal gland, or third eye, isn't getting the required darkness. This is a challenging area for caregivers to navigate. If you can obtain support to catch up on some sleep, it will help with the journey.

EVOLUTION AUTISTIC — Nicole Kretschmann

Chapter 7

HYPER VERSUS HYPO

Everything we touch, taste, smell, hear, or see is sensory input. Your child can be hypersensitive or hyposensitive to sensory input, or even both. Figuring this out will help you assist them in balancing back to their baseline. At the baseline, individuals can learn, process information, be at peace, and operate from their authentic selves. Most importantly, the individual can be emotionally regulated.

Some children will require less sensory input (hypersensitive), while others will require more sensory input (hyposensitive). The important thing to remember is that it is not your child's fault if they are unregulated. It is not their fault they can't get back to baseline alone. Your role is to help them and respect their sensory preferences. Here are some examples of adjustments we can make to accommodate both hyper and hypo sensitivities through the five standard senses:

1. Noise

Hyper–noise cancelling headphones, quiet spaces, silence, TVs and iPads on low volume settings, white noise to mask distracting sounds and ear plugs.

Hypo – playing the drums, loud music, high volume on learning devices, fidget toys that click.

2. Taste

Hyper–consistent and familiar food brands, not forcing foods, respecting texture preferences

Hypo–exposure to strong-tasting condiments such as hot sauces, spices, tangy juices, flavoured water

3. Smell

Hyper–fragrance-free personal and cleaning products, air purifiers, and good ventilation

Hypo – aromatherapy diffusers in the room, essential oil on collars, scented pens, markers and stress balls

4. Touch

Hyper-soft fabrics without tags or seams that can irritate the skin, cold or hot water preferences

Hypo–weighted blankets, compression stockings, compression vests

5. Sight

Hyper–Sunglasses, tinted eyewear for screentime, brimmed hats and visors

Hypo–visual input from spinning objects, patterns, bright colours, and bright lights.

Chapter 8

TELEPATHY

In ancient times, telepathy was often considered a typical or natural communication style among some cultures and belief systems. Unfortunately, these gifts have been suffocated through time and the busyness of our world. If you have an autistic child, there is a very high chance they are telepathic. Please pay attention. Don't dismiss, don't downplay, and don't think you're imagining things. These kids can read thoughts and sense events, particularly danger, at quite a young age. It has mostly remained a subject of speculation, interest, and debate in metaphysical contexts. Through conversations with other parents of autistic children and personal experiences with a range of autistic children, I can guarantee you that telepathy exists. It's certainly not limited to only autistic children, and it's just easier for them to tune in. For this chapter, I will document a few examples of my experience of telepathy with my children. It is most prevalent in my eldest son, whom I credit for coming into my higher dimension of intuitive gifts.

Our autistic children will have a strong sense of purpose or calling. They will have intuitive goals that contribute positively to the world. It's not usually to fulfil personal ambition but to collectively contribute to the Evolution of Earth through societal well-being. They play special roles. If allowed, you will witness them continually seeking ways to fulfil this by acting with compassion and passion in their pursuits, inspiring others to find deeper meaning and connection in their own lives.

When one of my sons was three years old, he was still non-verbal. He would take my hand and lead me to what he wanted if he wanted to communicate. He then started doing this for the things I wanted, even though I hadn't communicated them to him, only thought about them in my head. I would think about how much I would love a shower, and the next minute, he would pull me into the bathroom and push me into the shower. I would think about wanting to go for a drive in the car, and he would walk over to the car keys, pick them up, and place them in my hand.

I hired a nanny at home to help me with my son a couple of hours each week. He was very fixated on his interests, and I found it hard to spend time with my other child at the time, as he still didn't like being on his own; he liked a safe person nearby to share his interests. After interviewing many nannies, who were all met with cries and screams and 'get out of my space' indicators from him, I had almost given up. But Freda soon arrived on our doorstep for an interview. Not only did he immediately engage with her, he took her by the hand, sat her down on the lounge room floor, and sat on her lap. When he climbed up to kiss her on the cheek, I could not believe what I was witnessing. HIRED. The two had a beautiful soul connection. My son loved being in Freda's company, and she spent many years with us before leaving to go home to her country of the Solomon Islands.

One afternoon, Freda was bathing my son. He was four at this stage, and he started singing the happy birthday

Chapter 8 — TELEPATHY

song to her. It's interesting because he would never sing. Freda would later tell me it was actually her birthday, but she hadn't told us because she didn't want to make a big fuss. My son, however, deeply understood that it was her birthday without that being communicated to him by conventional means. It was a surprise to us that he knew the Happy Birthday song!

This leads me to my next story. I found out one of my sons could read one day when I took him into the wine shop to choose a bottle of wine. I picked up a bottle of Sav Blanc, which was branded Rock, Scissors, Paper. I later put it down as a replacement for a different brand. After paying for my purchase, my son turned to me and said, why didn't you buy one that Rock Paper Scissors wine? Interesting. I hadn't said it out loud. Observant and can read! Or was he just reading my thoughts as I read the label? Not sure. I reflected on it a lot. I even checked the next time I was at the shop to see if it had symbols of rock paper and scissors that maybe he had interpreted. It didn't. Interestingly, if you put a book in front of him and ask him to read, he wouldn't. Can he read? Definitely. He'll say out loud random words on shop labels or buildings. Does he want to read a book? No, but that's okay. He'll read what he is interested in when the time is right.

He also had a love of Freddo chocolates. So much so that on the days when we were out and about, he would always get a Freddo treat for the ride home. We visited the Chipmunks playground with one of his younger brothers on this particular day. They didn't sell Freddos, so I promised my son we'd stop at the corner shop on the way home and get them one each. On the drive home, my son reminded me 13246546513214654612 times that we needed to stop at the shop for his Freddo, so I didn't forget! Five minutes into the drive home, it started pouring rain. I would not say I like getting out of the car in the rain, but I knew I had promised him a Freddo. Against my better judgement, I tried negotiating with him, "Can we just drive through McDonald's so mummy doesn't have to get out of the rain." "No, mum, Maccas don't sell Freddos". So we continued, with me agreeing I would get out at the shop.

A few minutes later, I had a thought and a vision of a Freddo in the nappy bag, which made me realise that a few days before, I had packed some Freddos in the nappy bag for an outing that I hadn't handed out. Oh, thank god, I thought to myself, I'll have to pull over where I can and get it out of the nappy bag. A millisecond later, and I mean a millisecond later, I hear from the backseat, "Mum, get the Freddos out of the nappy bag". What? I almost crashed the car. I pulled over and turned around to the back seat when I could. "Can you read mummy's thoughts?" I asked. I had tears streaming down my face. I was met with the biggest of cheekiest smiles. "Mum, get my Freddo out of the bag". My mind was truly blown.

We were home one afternoon, just a normal afternoon; my eldest son was five at that stage. All of a sudden, out of absolutely nowhere, he started panicking. "Mummy, I'm scared, mummy, I'm scared, bad people, bad people are around". I tried getting him to elaborate, but he just kept walking around in circles, getting everyone inside the house, locking the doors, closing the windows, crying, telling me to call his dad, who was at work on nightshift and tell him to come home. He couldn't tell me why he was feeling this way; it was almost like he was on the verge of having a panic attack, but I couldn't decipher the trigger. I sent a message to my husband at work asking him to triple-check everything when he got home and ensure the house, shed, and gates were all safely locked. I reassured my son that I had relayed the message to his dad and that he would make sure we were all safe.

He waited that night, pacing, crying and anxious, constantly checking that the doors were locked and the curtains were closed until his dad got home from work. He then made sure he had witnessed his dad checking the security. He eventually fell asleep with the light on. The next day, he was fine; nothing was wrong, and his behaviours were normal. Our house was fine. I didn't mention anything because I didn't want to trigger anything. Two days later, our neighbour called me over to the fence. He let me know their house was broken into two nights earlier. I almost fainted. Please listen to your child; they know best.

One year, we had a cyclone heading straight for the city where we lived. It was predicted to cross the coastline as a Category 3 at 7 pm that night. As the winds started picking up around 6 pm, I was taking a video of us looking out the window and watching the trees sway. He turns to me and says, "1 o'clock, 1 o'clock is when it will be the worst". "1 am in the morning?" I ask. "Yes, mummy". I didn't really take too much notice of this as it was predicted to be all over by 9 pm. Which it was. My husband stayed up that night just in case. Just before midnight, the winds started picking up again, and we got annihilated from then until just before 2 am.

Interestingly, this is when we lost our trampoline, one of my son's favourite items. The cyclone had circled back, and winds were now blowing more heavily in the opposite direction. When I think he couldn't amaze me anymore, he does just that.

Many of you will be reading this thinking, no way; these children are just one-offs; my child doesn't have these gifts. If you pay enough attention and provide a safe and nurturing environment for your child, I assure you that you will start to notice things. When you do, document them; I wish I had started earlier. Slow it down and keep their environment free from much sensory input. Once there is too much or too much pressure on them, they can shut down entirely to drown out. Think of your normal volume input, for example. Say your normal input volume on the TV is at volume 10. Your sensory system might recognise this input as is 30/100 for your tolerance threshold. For an autistic child, the TV being at volume 10, may measure a sensory input of 100/100. So the TV just being on doesn't leave room to process anything else.

When one of my sons was two, he insisted I call a lady I worked with, Irene. "Call Irene, call Irene, call Irene", on repeat all morning. It was a Sunday morning, and I felt uneasy about calling and interrupting her over the weekend. After approximately 20 minutes, my boy became increasingly upset and heightened, screaming at me to call Irene. I had not seen him rise to such extreme emotion before over me making a call to someone. Nor had he requested to call Irene before. I asked him, "Why do you want mummy to call Irene?" With that, he ran outside, grabbed his Little Tikes car, and pushed it from behind straight into another toy car, yelling, "Crash,

crash, crash, crash, crash," he was begging me to call her. With that, I made the call. Not only was Irene driving a new vehicle on the highway from Cairns to Townsville, but she had also had a dream the night before that she had a car accident and was trapped behind an airbag. I explained what was happening to her before my son and Irene took the call seriously. We will never know if she was destined for a car accident that day. My intuition says exactly that. My son was instantly calm once he had heard me communicate the message to Irene.

I'm rehashing my particular experiences to make other parents aware so you are more alert of the messages coming through from your child. As autistic adults, most of the skills and openness we had as children are eroded. The new children coming through have higher-intelligent parents, so these won't be eroded. Be alert and be aware.

Chapter 9

REGULATE THE NERVOUS SYSTEM

Autistic individuals are very highly calibrated in their nervous systems. They have been here before. They are various forms of consciousness born into a body. Don't underestimate what they know and understand. It'll be more than you do; whether they can express this in a way you understand is another topic altogether.

I can't stress the importance of regulating their nervous systems. They are often bringing in prior life experiences of trauma and anxiety and, for that reason, will be naturally on guard. Until they can feel peace, safety, and security in every cell of their bodies, they will find it difficult to come into their talents or purposes for being here. Without a regulated nervous system, they will not achieve or do what they're here to do because fear and other outside forces will slow them from progressing. Most will find it in adulthood; however, if you can give them a head start, that's all the better for them.

Allow them to show up each day as they are, and you show up each day as you are. Everything begins to flow effortlessly and safely when this happens, and miracles will happen. Parents of autistic children need to free themselves from past programming and beliefs about what autism is and the identities associated with autism. It will be the key to your child's success.

Here are a few suggestions to help regulate the nervous system.

- Home school or alternate school.
- Secure attachment to parents.
- Gentle parenting.
- socialisation only when they are a willing participant.
- Co-sleeping.
- Safe, harmonious room.
- Positive Affirmations.
- Massage and brushing of skin.
- Don't force social norms.
- Tell them how lucky you are to have them.
- Be proud of them.
- Make sure they know they are loved.
- Child-led affection.
- Allow them to make decisions.
- Allow them a life of ease.

'Please remember that your child is your priority, not others'.

Our children are not interested in proving themselves. They have limitless consciousness, and they understand this. As parents, we have nothing to prove to others. Accept and love these children as they are. If that comes with judgment from family, friends or even strangers (trust me, it will), please ignore the judgment and move on. Please don't try to explain or be heard; most won't get it, as judgmental humans are generally stuck on lower levels of Evolution.

Most humans have been conditioned in this man-made environment, and to feel worthy, you must have qualifications, a career, family and marriage, physical appearance, financial status, and egotistical personal situations - the list continues. Autistic individuals are not interested in this, so please don't condition them to society's standards. They are far from it and far more advanced than this conditioning.

The majority of modern families have lost their power to time and money. Get it back. Nurture these kids yourself. You have been gifted with the role this lifetime. Please don't give it away to others, and don't give these incredible children away to be raised by others.

Within some cultures, when a child is diagnosed as being autistic, it comes with an element of devaluing the child. Being themselves is suddenly 'not enough'. When we own our Universe, the Creator, God, Source or whoever you call creating us, you can understand that no one or nothing is a mistake. They were likely designed to move into the next level of our Evolution and suit what's coming next for us all.

Their presence here comes with a purpose. They need to embody this, and you need to embrace it. Let them be more of themselves and less of what everyone else wants them to be. I remember we purchased hundreds of washing machines through the Facebook marketplace for two years to support my son's fixated interest. This is where he learnt to fix washing machines. It was his obsession and his passion. It was met with comments from others like, "You should encourage his interests elsewhere", "Your backyard looks like a dump", and "You shouldn't let him take things apart. It could be dangerous". They simply did not understand this is who he is and why he is here. An enjoyable life comes from living authentically and permitting your child to live as authentically as possible, regardless of the opinions of others and your past programming of how a child should be.

Teach your child that the power of their being is not subject to any limitations.

Chapter 10

PANS

The upgrade of DNA, cells, and genetic sequencing of humans on an earth that isn't evolving at the same pace can cause health problems for autistic children. One lesser-known co-occurring condition is an inflammatory response of the immune system and body, known as Paediatric Acute-onset Neuropsychiatric Syndrome (PANS).

Most autistic children have differing immune systems, not just differing brain wiring. PANS can be triggered by some form of infection. For one of my sons, it was triggered by contracting COVID-19. If your child does not fully recover from sickness and seems to regress developmentally, please don't dismiss this as the term many professionals like to label 'normal regressive autism'. Often, chronic inflammation occurs in their body that they cannot manage on their own. Familiarise yourself with the signs and symptoms of PANS so that if it happens, you can take action instead of relying solely on outdated information.

A changing immune system is part of the evolution process. Another important aspect to be aware of is that autistic children may react differently to many standard medications. Remember, you may need to administer lower doses than the standard for some common over-the-counter and prescription medications. A child with inflammation will often seek relief with cold water, whether that be through drinking, bathing or swimming. They will usually not feel the cold in their bodies as much as others and be fine with less clothing or no blankets.

Chapter 11

FUNDING

Should these incredible autistic children and their carers have access to government funding to support their nurturing, growth, and education? ABSOLUTELY. Our current systems are so dependent on having to constantly prove a child's "disability" to obtain funding that we start engaging in negative narratives. It also creates limiting beliefs we then adopt for our children. Humans have lost the art of recognising how powerful negative words are and what power they hold over their realities.

The process of obtaining government funding for these purposes should be automatic, fair, and guaranteed, ensuring that one or more carers can stay home from work duties and be able to homeschool if they choose to, providing and coordinating these extraordinary children with all the necessary education and therapy required to thrive in a society that has yet to fully accept, recognise and accommodate their needs.

Our current system is fundamentally flawed. I talk to many parents who fear losing funded supports if they don't report on how hard life is or how "delayed" their child is. This is a harmful practice. Parents or carers should not be put through this rigorous and demeaning process. They deserve more than what they currently receive. In the Country in which I reside, we have the

NDIA (National Disability Insurance Agency), which provides funding for some autistic individuals. While I am grateful for this scheme, it only scratches the surface of what is truly needed and views autism in an incorrect light, which only delays the collective shift and the purpose of these children. Autistic children should have their funding Scheme with a completely different pool of funds and labels.

It's vital that carers recognise their importance. You have been chosen for this. Autistic children have a unique perspective and potential that can and will significantly contribute to our future. In the meantime, they need the right support to navigate a world designed for neurotypical individuals. Parents and Carers are responsible for nurturing these children and helping them reach their full potential. This role is invaluable and irreplaceable.

Advocating for more substantial funding for autistic children and their carers is not just a necessity but a moral imperative. These children are key to our future, and their carers play a critical role in their missions being carried through. It is time for society to recognise this and ensure that the process of obtaining funding is straightforward and generous. Be brave, fight the battles, and stand tall in the unwavering belief and knowing that both you and your child deserve this support.

My opinion on this matter is not limited to autistic children. I believe all children and all carers should have access to the necessary funding required to shaping the future through our children. This is a topic for another discussion, perhaps in another book, but imagine the fantastic future for our planet if we prioritize appropriate funding for children and carers across the board. And in the not-distant future, neurotypical children will need further appropriate support to fit into an autistic-dominated world. Let us ensure it's an all-inclusive future. There is more than enough money available to make this a reality.

EVOLUTION AUTISTIC — Nicole Kretschmann

Chapter 12

THE 5TH DIMENSION

Before the birth of my first son, the idea of a 5th dimension hadn't even crossed my mind. I began to understand this extraordinary concept through my newfound spiritual gifts and teachings. The 5th dimension, characterised by love, unity, and a higher vibrational frequency, is a level of reality beyond our ordinary perceptions.

Transitioning to the 5th dimension involves a shift in consciousness and an awakening to a deeper understanding of oneself and one's connection to the Universe. From this elevated space, we can transcend the physical and embrace higher states of being, experiencing a realm beyond our everyday existence. This journey opens the door to a life filled with profound insights and boundless possibilities. Heaven on Earth. Earth has reached the point of so much destruction, so there will be separation to move into the new frequency and elevated vibration. Humans must be of a particular evolution and frequency to shift into the 5D.

My only hope is that you read this with an open mind. There will be a time in the future when this will make sense. In an autistic individual, the portals are open. There are more autistic people being born, and they are incarnating with 5th dimensional vibration. There is discord between the physical, also known as the 3rd dimension, and the ascending to the 5th dimension.

This is why the world can feel so alien to them. Autistic kids often observe 'normal' human behaviours. Some try to mimic these behaviours to fit in, while others stay true to themselves and are not interested in blending in. You'll recognise which one you have in your child.

Females on the spectrum often try to blend in and mask their true selves. They fake it, which makes it seem like there are fewer autistic girls, but really, they just fly under the radar more easily. Unfortunately, this comes at a high cost. Pretending to be something they're not can harm their soul, leading to a lifelong struggle with trauma, anxiety, and depression.

Our kids bring unique perspectives and incredible potential to our world. They remind us that being different is powerful and authenticity should be celebrated. It is our job, as parents, to stop placing the electric fences around these kids. They know their power; it's now your turn to understand it.

It's a gift, and it's not something that we need to fix. Often, navigating this field will require you to adopt limiting beliefs about your child. And much of the language necessary to get support and services for our kids in this field involves negativity. I can assure you that your child is special and here for a reason.

It's not a mistake, and it's not a punishment. Autistic tendencies are tools to navigate through the ever-changing world. With the mission of helping the collective ascend.

Planet Earth has evolved by pulling vibration into its core. It's no different for humans.

If I had to categorise a set of traits for autistic people at the core, it would be this. It also includes those individuals who can shift into other dimensions. These people may be autistic and not realise it. Many adults are now realising that they are autistic, and often, this comes after the diagnosis of their child. Most of them reflect knowing that they've always felt different, thought differently, and felt differently.

One of the key characteristics of autism is the profuse talking about subjects they are passionate about. This is widely misunderstood, mainly from my experience. There are not many topics I talk about. However, when I'm on a roll about an area of interest, eg Evolution of autism, I'm not following social cues or allowing others to talk, not because I don't understand social cues. It's that often because I am channelling information, I can't stop. I block out a lot so I don't miss anything. From my experience as a channeller, I can say that you don't have the choice to cut it off and pause it; it all comes out at once, and I have to get it all out, or I lose it. And it is important!

My spirit guides want all to understand that you don't need to know someone autistic or from a higher dimension to get to the 5th dimension. We're all capable, and as we all have consciousness, it's easier for those who vibrate at a higher frequency. We all can access higher consciousness. We live in a multidimensional world, and I would assume that if you are reading this book, you are likely already familiar with other dimensions and aware that we never truly die. Our consciousness simply transitions.

These signs reflect the expansion of consciousness and alignment with universal love, compassion, and purpose, guiding individuals towards profound self-exploration and contribution to humanity's Evolution.

I believe this set of traits better describes an autistic individual.

Increased Empathy and Compassion: Feeling more connected to other's emotions, wanting to help and improve everyone's well-being.

Improved Senses: Experiencing the world in a richer, more detailed way, sensing energy around you.

Inner Peace: Finding deep peace inside, feeling more aligned with a higher state of being.

Better Intuition: Can make decisions based on a strong inner sense of what's right, beyond just logical thinking.

Blended Senses: Experiences senses mixing, like seeing colours when hearing sounds.

Connection with Nature: Feeling more in sync with nature, noticing meaningful coincidences that guide you.

Flexible Sense of Time: Time feels more fluid, helping them to appreciate the present moment more.

Less Focus on Ego: Care less about external approvals or material things and focus on inner fulfilment.

Telepathic Connections: Communicate nonverbally with others in a similar heightened state of awareness.

Visions: See intricate patterns and symbols. It can be in everyday life, during meditation or dreams, noticing more details.

Enhanced Psychic Abilities: Stronger abilities like seeing the future or understanding things beyond normal senses.

Unconditional Love: Love and accept themselves and others without conditions, contributing to personal and collective growth.

CONCLUSION

As the chosen ones, fitting in was never our destiny, so let's celebrate our differences, honour our truths, and radiate authenticity. In a world of conformity, be the vibrant colours that light up the mosaic of lifeforce. Let's boldly embrace our individuality, stand tall in our truth, and illuminate the world with brilliance. Autistic individuals are the future; they are our guides and awaiting destiny. Let's strive to be more like them. They bring unique perspectives, incredible talents, and boundless creativity. As a parent, you have been given your most important job yet. Embrace this journey and be grateful that you were chosen for this opportunity.

ABOUT THE AUTHOR

Nicole Kretschmann is an author dedicated to fostering positive relationships with autistic individuals and reshaping the narrative around their differences. She believes there is no room for limiting beliefs about autism in our society. As a neurodivergent individual, Nicole is well-educated in autism and is currently pursuing a research master's degree. She also holds qualifications in accounting and energy work.

Since the birth of her first son, Nicole's ability to communicate using the senses beyond the physical realm has significantly increased, manifesting as claircognisance, clairsentience, clairvoyance, and clairaudience. She now uses her heightened sensitivities for the benefit of all. Her proudest and most important achievement is being a mother to four beautiful and talented neurodivergent sons.

"I honour my truth and express my views on the evolution of autism through many channels," she says.

By combining science, spirituality, strategy, and a connection to a higher power, Nicole is bringing a new awareness to the evolutionary process we call autism, changing how we view the mind, body and soul connection for the greater good of all.

Notes

Notes:

Notes

Notes

Notes

www.ingramcontent.com/pod-product-compliance
Lightning Source LLC
Chambersburg PA
CBHW061740070526
44585CB00024B/2760